Lotte's War

Lotte's War

Bunkers, Bombs and Barrage Balloons

by Lotte Moore

URBANE
Publications

urbanepublications.com

First published in Great Britain in 2016
by Urbane Publications Ltd
Suite 3, Brown Europe House, 33/34 Gleaming Wood Drive,
Chatham, Kent ME5 8RZ
Copyright ©Lotte Moore, 2016

A CIP catalogue record for this book is available
from the British Library.

ISBN 978-1-911331-57-5
MOBI 978-1-911331-58-2

Design and Typeset by Michelle Morgan
Cover design by Michelle Morgan. Illustration by Philip Hood.

Cover by Julie Martin

Printed and bound by CPI Group (UK) Ltd, Croydon, CR0 4YY

urbanepublications.com

Many thanks to Diana Elderton for her invaluable research and help.

Thank you to Philip Hood for his wonderful illustrations.

For Johnny

by John Pudney

Do not despair
For Johnny-head-in-air;
He sleeps as sound
As Johnny underground.
Fetch out no shroud
For Johnny-in-the-cloud;
And keep your tears
For him in after years.

Better by far
For Johnny-the-bright-star,
To keep your head,
And see his children fed.

In 1940 my father, John Pudney, was commissioned into the Royal Air Force as an intelligence officer and as a member of the Air Ministry's Creative Writer's Unit. During World War II he published articles for this organization and wrote a lot of poetry, including this famous ode to British airmen, 'For Johnny'. This poem achieved national significance and was broadcast and performed by several famous actors, including Sir Laurence Olivier and Sir John Mills.

A CHILD'S WAR

Before the bombs

When I arrived in this world in a Maida Vale clinic on 15th March 1936, my Dad couldn't see me, his first born, as he had severe measles.

My earliest memories are of being at our Essex farmhouse which we moved to just before the war. The house was surrounded by cornfields and several barns, one of which had about twenty cows who were milked by hand every day by milkmen sitting on stools. They always had the wireless on because cows love music.

Our house was quite dark, there was no electricity so there were candles in every room and also some little smoky lamps. I remember Mum often asking one of the farm workers to get some water because our taps didn't work. He walked across the fields to the 'ram' (a pump) where rainwater was collected in a tank. We washed at night from a jug of warm water which was poured into an enamel bowl.

Everyone was friendly on the farm. The milk was collected in big urns and delivered to the villages. The farmhands made butter and cheese and the ladies made bread and cakes. The men also made beer.

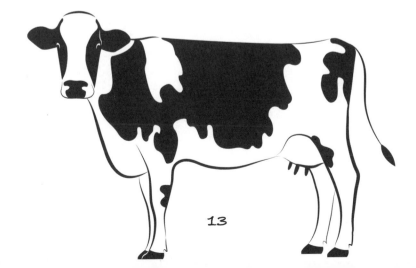

We had many walks through the cornfields
into lovely woods playing hide-and-seek, and
follow-my-leader. Dad taught us the names
of the trees and flowers and of the vegetables
that he grew. Our chickens gave us lots of
eggs which we collected every day in a basket.
Sometimes we saw baby chicks hatching from
their shells

A picture of me with my Dad and Farmer Ted

"We'll have lots to eat this winter, won't we Mother?"

Grow your own
Can your own

During the war, rationing meant that lots of people grew their own food – living in the country meant we were already used to growing and storing a lot of food.

After we had been in the farmhouse for about a year, electricity finally arrived and the house became much lighter.

We had log fires and Mum was excited at having a fridge to keep food safely because she only had a larder before and food often went bad.

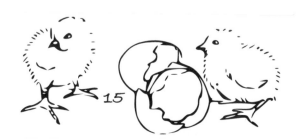

In the winter the snow was often very thick and our big pond had so much ice on it that we learned to skate pushing a chair to hold us up. Such fun. There was no TV, no telephone, just a radiogram playing records and Mummy played the piano for us to sing and dance to.

One day, Dad told us that Mum was going to have a baby. We'd seen our white cat give birth to five kittens in Mum's hat-box under the spare-room bed and assumed that she was going to do the same.

We rushed over to the cowshed and told Bill, the head cow-man,

"Our Mum's going to have a baby under the bed."

He was busy milking the cows and just laughed.

A few weeks later Dad was given a funny old donkey called Bella who we loved playing with. She was very naughty, sometimes eating Dad's favourite flowers. One day we found her in the kitchen eating some bread. Another day we found her eating candles on the piano!

The Barrage Balloons appear

It was a very happy time until life suddenly changed and I didn't understand why.

One morning I looked out of my bedroom window and there were some great big, ugly, grey 'barrage' balloons hanging in the air above the lovely fields where rabbits and foxes used to play.

Lots of men on the farm looked worried and were huddled together, muttering. Some kept looking up at the sky. It was September 1939 and Dad told me a war with Germany had begun.

In May 1940, the Germans had invaded France, nearly capturing the British army that had been sent to help the French people.

But unknown to the Germans hundreds of boats, big and small, hurried across the English Channel to take on board the English soldiers and bring them home.

Despite desperate fighting and bombing most of our soldiers were rescued. Dad told me that several of his friends who owned boats crossed over to Dunkirk and brought back our men through all the shelling and bombing. The wounded were sent to hospitals and when they recovered enough they taught newly conscripted soldiers how to fight.

The courageous actions of hundreds of boat owners saved the lives of thousands of soldiers from the British Expeditionary Force

My Dad, Squadron Leader Pudney

We had an old radio which Mum and Dad always listened to with serious faces. My brother Jeremy, who was eighteen months at the time, often screamed when some noisy airplanes flew over our house.

Dad told me the horrid balloons were there to protect us.

"From what?" I asked.

I knew little about the war starting, and that Dad would be disappearing to join the Royal Air Force and help fight against a man called Hitler in Germany.

A few weeks later some American airmen knocked on the door. They looked so funny as they were in their pyjamas and holding toothbrushes. Mum told them where the bathroom was and about twenty smiling men queued up.

American airmen flew lots of bombing raids from British airfields in WWII

The Americans were Britain's allies, and the airmen were living in tents at a nearby aerodrome and didn't have running water to wash in.

They were very jokey and after a few days started handing out 'candy' (sweets) and chewing-gum to us which was a great treat.

I never realized these brave men were going to fly over Germany. Some were shot down in their airplanes and never came back.

Leaving home

After my fifth birthday in 1941, my home
life disappeared and with it much of my
childhood freedom. No more happy rambles
in the woods, or enjoying the wildlife, or
pond-skating when the ice was thick.

Why? Because my parents had decided I
should go to a country boarding school called
Langford Grove in Herefordshire (near
Wales) where their friend, Mrs Curtis, was the
friendly headmistress.

It would be a safe place, miles away from the dangers of war.

Children
As children were being evacuated they had labels attached to them, as though they were parcels.

Gas Masks
A year before the war began, the British government handed out 40 million gas masks.

So, I was 'evacuated' like many other children. All the evacuees had to carry a gasmask in a box and a small carrier bag filled with their most precious possessions. Everyone had an identity card to prove who they were. I felt

Many children were evacuated during WWII to keep them safe from bombing

sorry for some children who were evacuated to elderly couples where there were no toys or books. Many children were also evacuated on ships to the USA, Canada or Australia.

Arriving at a tall old building surrounded by fields, lakes and a big garden, we were shown to our dormitory. Each of us had a locker where we put our few special toys and books.

Saying goodbye to Mum and Dad (who'd driven me there) was so sad. We sobbed and howled as we watched our parents disappear up a long, long drive while we frantically waved goodbye.

Even though we were all very homesick, overwhelmed and vulnerable, the many outdoor activities kept us distracted and busy.

There was swimming in the lake (often without a costume), rescuing baby owls, singing around a log fire while Mrs Curtis - or 'Curtie' as we called her -

gave us new songs to learn for Christmas. She also read lots of stories to us after supper.

Mrs Curtis had messy long hair, big bulging eyes and a huge mouth which sometimes shouted so loud we thought she would gobble us up. We used to play dangerous games in the big dormitory (six floors up) called 'Truth, Dare and Promise'. If someone dared you to stand on the window ledge YOU HAD TO DO IT!

I did it once, and looking down at the pebbly drive I don't know how I didn't fall.

Another time I was dared with two girls to drop a toilet roll down six flights of stairs, so it ended up right in front of Curtie's study!

Matron was very cross, not just because it was a naughty prank, but because toilet roll was so precious!

Virol was advertised everywhere and recommended for all children

When the bell rang we had to queue-up for our disgusting medicine - 'Scott's Emulsion', a white, thick and slimy fluid. Then Virol, which was dark brown and tasted like oozy mud. These medicines were full of vitamins to keep us healthy.

I don't remember doing many lessons, but we learned to enjoy music (not least by playing the recorder). The older children played the piano and there was lots of singing which always made us happy. There was no entertainment we could look at so we made up plays or danced.

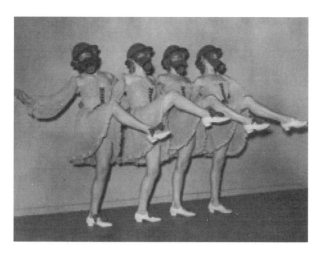

I'm glad we didn't have to dance
in our gas masks!

Sometimes I got a postcard from Mum and Dad and scribbled back a tiny picture (not having learned to write properly). To save paper we sent letters back using a sticky address label.

Some food was really yucky. Our tapioca pudding was disgusting and we called it 'frogspawn'. It was white and blobby and we held our noses when we swallowed it down with a drink of water.

There was also Spam, which was like eating slabs of pink plastic - proper meat was incredibly rare. The corned beef we ate came out of a huge tin. Burgers or fishfingers hadn't been invented.

The school had a big vegetable garden so we were made to each spinach and leeks (which we didn't enjoy), but we lapped up the carrots, potatoes and peas. We had no butter, only margarine. At break times we had lovely 'dripping' (which is like gravy) on hot toast. Bread was made by the cooks. It was soft brown because white flour was scarce.

The government tried to encourage everyone to grow food. By growing our own vegetables, we were helping the war effort.

We never knew where the bombs might land next...

The one event we dreaded was fire practice. We queued-up on the top floor, then stepped through the open window into a big, long, brown sack and were told to push out our knees and elbows as we whizzed down the dark tunnel. We were caught at the bottom by two firemen holding a blanket.

Fire practice was very important during the war because if a house was bombed it would very likely catch fire, making it difficult to escape.

Another unpleasant event was hair inspection every week in case we had 'nits' (hair lice).

If you had long hair you tied it back in bunches with ribbon or plaited it so you were less likely to get head lice. If you did get them your hair was washed in soft brown soap, then while leaning over a newspaper it was combed with a very fine metal comb to get the nits out. It could be quite painful, especially if you had long hair. If you sat close to someone, the nits could jump onto another head very easily, so we often had them!

My little sister Tessa. This picture was taken after the war was over.

After a few months, Curtie called me into her cosy room to tell me Mummy had given birth to my baby sister.

She had her under the stairs in a cupboard because she couldn't get to the air-raid shelter in time. I was happy and sad at the same time because I wanted to see the baby straight away but only had a photo to look at.

I wondered if she would have to wear a gas mask? Mrs Curtis told me they had a sort of veil to protect them. I started crying because I wanted to go home. Mrs Curtis sat me on her lap and told me a funny story which made me laugh. Later I ran off to tell my friends about Tessa, my new sister.

Me and my younger
brother Jeremy

Eventually my brother Jeremy also came to
Langford Grove. It was lovely having him
there, but he only lasted a few weeks. He was
swinging on a tree when the branch snapped
and he broke his arm – he was then sent home
(lucky thing!).

I often cried myself to sleep, so did some of
my friends. We wanted to go home so badly
and see our mums and dads.

We didn't understand what the war meant
because no one explained why we never saw
any airplanes or soldiers or heard any bombs

or air-raids. Deep in the countryside we were innocently playing and living with nature and creating our own fun in total safety.

It must have been terrible for many children because they were evacuated abroad. They had to travel sometimes for several weeks on big ships and arrived in a strange country. Can you imagine how tough that was!

Living through the War

Most dads went to help fight in the war and many mums became nurses to help the injured, or they worked in factories.

One of my aunts became a 'landgirl' and drove a tractor and ploughed the fields. Later she went up north and worked in a torpedo factory. Other women drove ambulances.

While I was staying in Herefordshire, one of the greatest events was when my lovely Granny came to collect me for a train journey to Hammersmith, and her home by the Thames.

I was very frightened as we walked back
from the tube station in the pitch dark, with
Granny holding a torch low over our feet.

Suddenly I smelled burning and as she hauled
me to the other side of the road I saw the
smouldering ruins of a house, flattened by a
bombing raid.

Members of the British Women's Land Army –
landgirls did vital work to keep Britain's crops
growing.

It was horrid and I wondered what happened to the poor people inside ~ were they dead or safe in an air-raid shelter? I didn't ask Granny, but I couldn't get the thoughts from my head. I tried not to cry holding Granny's hand very tightly.

When we got to Granny's house it was incredibly dark with only candlelight in each room which made it rather spooky.

"Don't open the 'blackout' curtains (the special black material over every window). It's not safe. The German aircraft must not see the light from our houses."

I could hear a 'chug- chug' noise as the old tugs towed some cargo boats up the river laden with coal, sugar and timber; I so wanted to peep out and see them.

When there was a bombing raid in London bright search-lights like white pencils in the sky searched for enemy planes so that the anti-aircraft guns could shoot them down.

I couldn't get used to the dark everywhere because at boarding school we never drew the big curtains in our dormitories at night

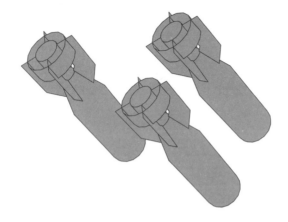

and we saw the moon peeping at us in bed, and then the sun bursting across the fields in daytime.

But here in London sometimes we heard planes zooming over. Grandpa knew if it was one of our planes by its special noise.

The Germans had 'dive bombers' which swooped down to let their bombs go. You couldn't mistake the noise they made.

A.P. Herbert, my dear grandfather, played a vital part during the war. He had a boat called The Water Gypsy which was used to guard against dangers in the river Thames.

He'd been in the Navy in World War 1 (1914 – 1918) so was asked to navigate his boat down to the House of Commons where he would meet the Prime Minister, Winston Churchill, and discuss ways of stopping enemy planes attacking the river.

My grandfather surrounded by his family

He had a special role training many local volunteers, mums, dads, policemen and shopkeepers to stand guard at night in the pitch dark along the riverbank to watch out for enemy planes coming over and trying to drop mines in the Thames by parachute.

He organized many local volunteers to alert the ships of this great hazard. The parachutes dropped gently into the river and no boat would know about the danger until it was too late and the mines exploded.

Every volunteer watched through the night and if he spotted a parachute he'd send a signal to my grandfather who'd warn any craft to steer clear.

Churchill said later, "You deserve a medal, Alan, for saving so many lives."

The volunteers were just ordinary folk all giving their services bravely, like so many thousands of others, helping out in any way they could.

The anxiety and threat of war brought out many peoples' generosity of spirit. Some men joined the A.R.P. (Air-Raid Precautions) and their jobs were to patrol the streets and make sure nobody was showing any lights through the windows ~ that's why we had blackout material. The wardens also helped anyone injured during raids and called ambulances and fire engines if a house caught fire.

Two years later in 1943, our family decided to move to Kent which was safer. I remember the excitement as our car was packed, including our white cat, six kittens, some baby chicks and my cage of white mice.

The new house on a hill in the village of Chipstead was old with a huge garden. Underneath were some enormous caves which were soon put to use as an air-raid shelter.

I was now seven and more aware of the
terrible war. I was made to wear a horrible
gas-mask whenever the air-raid siren went off.
Suddenly a group of planes zoomed overhead
and Mum took us down steep stone stairs
to the caves where lots of the local villagers
rushed to safety before the bombs fell.

It was very cold, damp and dark. Everyone
brought candles or torches with little paraffin
stoves to keep us warm, food, and thermos
flasks of tea which we all shared.

I was very frightened and often screamed as
we rushed down the staircase, because for
some reason I thought Hitler was going to
get me down there.

The gas-masks were tight and ugly so you couldn't hear people talking. Someone had a radio which told us the news, about Grandpa's friend Winston Churchill and what the Germans were trying to do.

We children played Snakes and Ladders, skipping games, and Hide and Seek in the damp, dripping spaces at the back of the caves.

We got so used to being down there that after a few months we even began sleeping there. Everyone was very friendly but sometimes I could hear people crying. One of my friends screamed when she heard her school was in flames.

One night a man rushed in yelling "She's gone, she's gone! My mum's house is on fire. She's dead!"

If they had nowhere to go, Mum offered to let people like him stay with us.

A sweet old man one day came into the cave with blood all down his arms crying that his wife had collapsed. Then another sad time we heard an explosion and a woman came rushing in screaming "My husband's plane went down." Everyone crowded around her.

A little boy I knew called Billy asked me, "What's a husband?"

"It's a dad," I said, hoping mine was alright in his plane miles away.

A ration book

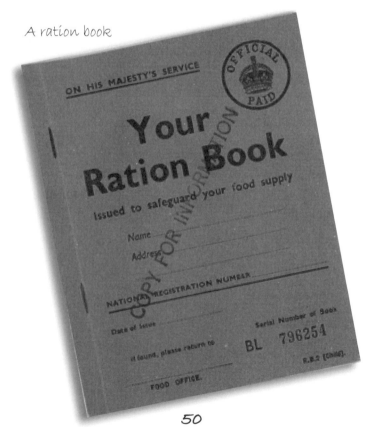

"I ain't got a dad anyway. Never had one. I'm only five," Billy added.

When the 'All Clear' sounded and everyone climbed out, we children asked for our 'sweet coupons' (you got four squares each for a week – they were very precious). When we eventually rushed into the sweet shop, the doorbell would clang and Rose (who worked in the shop) would say "Now, no queue barging! Wait your turn."

We were drooling at the sight of huge jars on the counter stuffed with different kinds of sweets. Eventually Rose gave us four ounces each in a paper bag. We walked down the cobbled pavement, scoffing the lot or swapping toffee for sherbert or lemon drops for liquorice sticks.

It wasn't just sweets that were rare, either. Everybody had a 'ration book' which contained coupons which were very small squares of paper, one for each week for basic needs like cheese, margarine, butter, bacon, porridge, wheat flakes, shredded wheat, lard, sugar, eggs, soap, sugar, washing powder, clothes and paper.

There were no supermarkets in those days. Shopping was bought at individual shops from the green-grocer, butcher, baker, fishmonger and grocer. People served you behind a counter and weighed everything before putting the goods in a paper bag. Biscuits were served loose from big tins and any broken ones were sold cheaper.

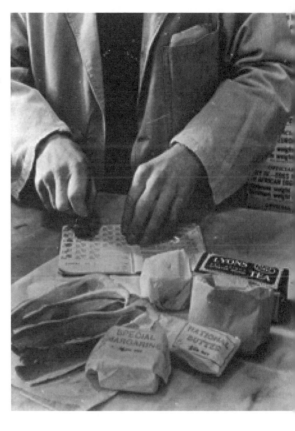

Shopkeepers collected coupons from customers

You gave coupons for everything. No one had a freezer and very few even had a fridge, so shopping was done every day to buy fresh food and only fruit and vegetables were more freely available as they were home-grown. Many people dug up their lawns to do this.

There was no frozen food or readymade meals like pizza, burgers, fishfingers or chicken nuggets. Rationing didn't finish until 1954, nearly ten years after the war ended.

The milkman (or woman) delivered bottles of milk every day from a horse-drawn cart and at schools every child had a small bottle of milk free.

Some people kept chickens and enjoyed the eggs (and later the chickens). Some families kept rabbits and cooked them in stews. The skins were treated and the fur sent away to make gloves or mittens.

There were metal dustbins on the roadside where any scraps of food or vegetable peelings were collected and taken to feed pigs on the farms.

The metal railings in front of all the houses were melted down to make weapons for the war.

Coal, which was normally used to heat houses, was delivered in sacks drawn by horse-drawn carts. The sacks were emptied into the coal cellar in the yard or under the pavement.

My brother and his friends used to run out when they heard the coalman and jump on the back of the cart laughing as they went for a long ride round the houses and along the narrow alleys. They were told off by their mums when they ran home covered in coal dust.

Another important person in those days was the chimney sweep who stuck brushes on long rods up the chimney to clear out the soot so the fires drew better. Years ago young boys were put up the wide chimneys to clean them by hand! (A friend of my brother's actually did this. He came from a very poor family who needed the money).

Houses were very cold with only one fire, and the bedrooms were freezing. We had to wear lots of extra clothes and some lucky people had hot-water-bottles sometimes made of stone and very heavy.

There was no toilet paper, so we had to cut up newspaper into squares and hang them on a piece of string. Sometimes, after eating oranges we used the tissue-paper they'd been wrapped in, which was softer.

Nothing was thrown away if it could be mended. Shoes went to the cobblers for new heels. Many clothes were second hand, some handed down from older children or swapped with other families. 'Make do and mend' was the motto. Some mums knitted jumpers and socks. Sometimes they'd unravel a worn jumper and knit a new one. Many people made their own, dresses, shirts, curtains, nighties - all sorts of things. We weren't fashion-conscious during the war; we wore anything. In fact, my husband, Chris, had to wear his sister's raincoat, which he hated because it buttoned up the wrong side.

The bread queue at the bakery was long on Mondays. I remember the wonderful smell of apple pies as I waited. Then it would be on to the butcher's. During this time, we had two lovely Alsatian dogs, Juno and Bobsy, who'd sometimes follow us there.

The owner, who was called Blake, was a huge, round, jolly man who always made jokes to the long queue of ladies waiting for their small ration of meat. He often kept a bone each for Juno and Bobsy who ran home with it in their mouths.

The fighting comes to an end

My Dad was a 'Squadron Leader' in the Royal Air Force. He also talked to pilots after they'd returned from bombing raids over Germany to find out where the Nazis stored their planes.

My father John Pudney broadcasting during the war and telling people about what was happening

Bombs destroyed so much and made many roads impassable

When he was at home he'd let me curl up in his fur-lined flying jacket, and I'd fall asleep.

Many schools in London were closed because it was the biggest target for the Germans to bomb, but in the country, quite a few stayed open, although lots of the teachers were away doing war work.

The terrible blitz destroyed so much of several cities such as Coventry, Plymouth, Manchester and London.

In June 1944 the Germans started using a new weapon, the 'Doodle-Bug'. It was like a bomb with wings. Some said it sounded like a lorry engine going very fast. When it ran out of fuel it turned down and crashed to the ground and exploded.

Later the Germans started using another new weapon, the V2. These were rockets that went so high that you couldn't hear them coming until they exploded on the ground.

This is why bunkers – and what were often called 'Anderson Shelters' - were so vital. These shelters were half buried in the ground with earth heaped on top to protect them from bomb blasts. They were made from six corrugated iron sheets bolted together at

the top, with steel plates at either end, and
measured 6ft 6in by 4ft 6in (1.95m by 1.35m).

Although often made from wood and tin
and built in a hole in peoples' gardens, they
could genuinely save lives when the bombs
were dropping.

After D-Day, on June 6th 1944, when the Allied armies landed in France, the British and American and Russian armies gradually advanced into Germany.

Hitler realized he was beaten and shot himself while in his command bunker in Berlin in May 1945.

As a child I didn't hear about any of these events and only later learned about them from my Dad.

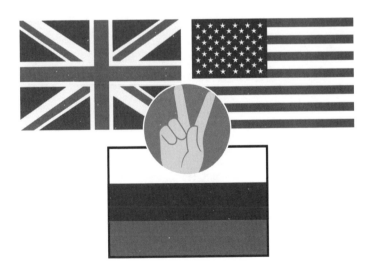

The war ended on VE Day (Victory Europe Day), the 8th May 1945. The whole country exploded into huge, happy street parties cheering for freedom and an end to all the bombing.

Church bells rang out up and down the land, bonfires were lit burning stuffed models of Hitler, and Churchill made a wonderful speech praising everyone for their great efforts achieved under his guidance.

What a fantastic leader Churchill was.
Little did my brother know he'd one day be
swimming in a pool at Chartwell and nearly
dive bomb him.

My best memory was running to Dad as he
walked through the gate without his uniform
as I then knew the war was over and he would
be staying home.

Sir Winston Churchill

COMMEMORATIONS

by John Pudney

Commemorations and names,
As we grow old,
With our dates for battles and for dames
Have all been told.

In between the death of friends
Our story went
Endlessly outspun, to make amends
For what was spent.

Endlessly a solemn tale
Of glory runs,
From the men who had the world for sale
To their sold sons.

World War II Timeline

1939

Hitler invades Poland on 1 September. Britain and France declare war on Germany two days later.

1940

Rationing starts in the UK.
German 'Blitzkrieg' overwhelms Belgium, Holland and France.
Churchill becomes Prime Minister of Britain.
British Expeditionary Force evacuated from Dunkirk.

British victory in Battle of Britain forces
Hitler to postpone invasion plans.

1941

Hitler begins Operation Barbarossa - the
invasion of Russia.
The Blitz continues against Britain's major
cities.
Allies take Tobruk in North Africa, and resist
German attacks.
Japan attacks Pearl Harbor, and the US enters
the war.

1942

Germany suffers setbacks at Stalingrad and El
Alamein.
Singapore falls to the Japanese in February -
around 25,000 prisoners taken.
American naval victory at Battle of Midway,
in June, marks turning point in Pacific War.

1943

Surrender at Stalingrad marks Germany's first major defeat.

Allied victory in North Africa enables invasion of Italy to be launched.

Italy surrenders, but Germany takes over the battle.

British and Indian forces fight Japanese in Burma.

1944

Allies land at Anzio and bomb monastery at Monte Cassino.

Soviet offensive gathers pace in Eastern Europe.

D Day: The Allied invasion of France. Paris is liberated in August.

Guam liberated by the US Okinawa, and Iwo Jima bombed.

1945

Russians reach Berlin: Hitler commits suicide and Germany surrenders on 7 May.
Truman becomes President of the US on Roosevelt's death, and Attlee replaces Churchill.
After atomic bombs are dropped on Hiroshima and Nagasaki, Japan surrenders on 14 August.

Lotte enjoys giving talks on her wartime experiences to schools and the response is always overwhelmingly enthusiastic!

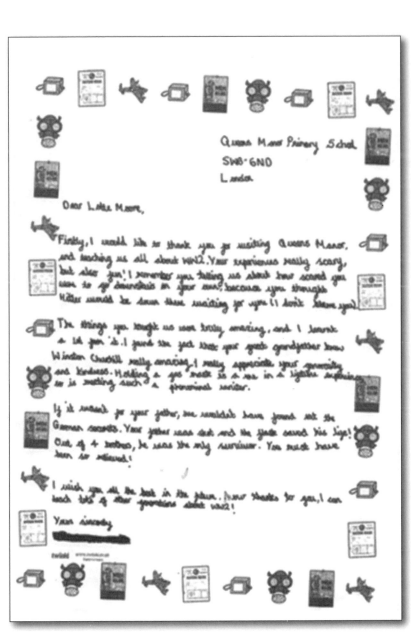

Queens Manor Primary School
SW8 6ND
London

Dear Luke Moore,

Firstly, I would like to thank you for visiting Queens Manor, and teaching us all about WW2. Your experiences really scary, but also fun! I remember you telling us about how scared you were to go downstairs in your own, because you thought Hitler would be down there waiting for you (I don't blame you).

The things you taught us were totally amazing, and I learnt a lot from it. I found the fact that your great grandfather knew Winston Churchill really amazing. I really appreciate your generosity and kindness. Holding a gas mask is a rare in a lifetime experience so is meeting such a prominent soldier.

If it wasn't for your father, we wouldn't have found out the German secrets. Your father was deaf and the flash saved his life! Out of 4 brothers, he was the only survivor. You must have been so relieved!

I wish you all the best in the future. From thanks for you, I can teach lots of other generations about WW2!

Yours sincerely,

twinkl   www.twinkl.co.uk

If you'd like Lotte to come to your school to talk about *Lotte's War,* or to read from one of her many children's books, you can reach her on

lotte@hamter.net

Lotte Moore is an 80-year-old writer on a mission. Her myriad children's stories have been enjoyed by primary school boys and girls around the country, particularly when they get a visit from Lotte, during which she inspires the children with her readings, and wartime stories of rationing and bombings. Lotte has written more than 16 books including her autobiography Snippets of a Lifetime. Despite writing stories since her childhood, Lotte only blossomed as a writer in her 70s. She was born into an incredibly literary family. Her father, John Pudney, wrote poetry (including the popular WW2 poem 'For Johnny'), novels and biographies. Her grandfather, Sir Alan Herbert, was a prolific writer, satirist and librettist.

As a child, Lotte lived in Kent with her parents who enjoyed entertaining, political debate and literary discussion with the likes of Charlie Chaplin, Winston Churchill, H E Bates, W H Auden and Benjamin Britten. During the war, having been evacuated, and then at school, Lotte often found herself feeling lonely and turned to writing (stories, diary, poems and letters) to express her feelings of isolation. In her early teens Lotte's commitment turned to ballet, and point shoes replaced the pen. She was selected by the Royal Ballet School to dance in the Opera Ballet. When rejected for growing 'too tall' Lotte turned to acting and intermittently to writing. She finally married aged 38 to her loyal husband Chris (who

continues to support Lotte in
many ways including typing out her
hand-written stories). Sadly, her parents
died before her writing career flourished.
Lotte lives in London, on the River Thames.